THE
RECRUITING
SURVIVAL
GUIDE

Chuck Mooney

21st Century Press
Fort Worth, Texas

© 1991 by Chuck Mooney

All rights reserved

No part of this book may be reproduced in any form or by any means, electronic or mechanical, including photocopying and recording, or by any information storage and retrieval system.

Printed in the United States of America

For information address

Chuck Mooney
P.O. Box 20174
Fort Worth, TX 76102-8174

ISBN 0-9630239-0 $9.95

Production and Printing coordinated by 21st Century Press
in conjunction with Landslyd Productions.

WITHDRAWN

796.332 Mo
Mooney, Chuck.
The recruiting survival
guide

14 DAY LOAN

DEC 4 1992

NEWARK PUBLIC LIBRARY
NEWARK, OHIO

STACKS

Special thanks to Kelly Bucheit for her late-night editing and endless support, to Lance & Hap Lyda for helping get this bird off the ground, to Kyle Swan whose illustrations lend the project credibility, to the good Lord for giving me a chance to play ball and write this book, and last but not least, my family for their friendship and inspiration.

CONTENTS

INTRODUCTION

CHAPTER 1
To The Athlete......................3

CHAPTER 2
To The Parents......................7

CHAPTER 3
Your Recruiter......................13

CHAPTER 4
The Head Coach......................19

CHAPTER 5
Get A Calendar......................23

Chapter 6
Discerning Truth From Flattery........25

Chapter 7
The Rating Services............................29

Chapter 8
Illegal Recruiting................................33

Chapter 9
The Visit..39

Chapter 10
Steroids..49

Chapter 11
Taking Care of the Homefront..........53

Chapter 12
Alumni...57

Chapter 13
Summer Jobs......................................61

Chapter 14
Handling the Press............................63

Chapter 15
Saying "No"...67

Chapter 16
Second Level Players........................71

Chapter 17
Redshirting..75

```
796.332 Mo
Mooney, Chuck.
 The recruiting survival
  guide
                   00217-6460
```

CHAPTER 18
Academics..79

CHAPTER 19
Making the Actual Decision..............83

CHAPTER 20
Signing Date..89

CHAPTER 21
After It's Over.....................................91

CHAPTER 22
Thank-You Notes................................95

CHAPTER 23
Getting Ready for Your Future.........97

THE RECRUITING SURVIVAL GUIDE

INTRODUCTION

The purpose of this book is to give the readers a grasp of just what it is that they are about to get into. Whether as a recruit or parent, the recruiting process can be a wonderful experience if handled properly and maturely. But, a word of caution: If you let it get out of control, it can become a nightmare.

This book is mainly aimed at the athlete, with some attention to the parents. This may be the first exposure to the recruiting world for the majority of readers, so I hope the book can be a helpful tool in the decision making process. This is also probably the first time you will undergo such a potentially stressful endeavor. Therefore, I will take you from square one right up to the signing date and beyond. My aim as the author is to give an unbiased view of what you are about to experi-

The Recruiting Survival Guide

ence, or quite possibly may already be going through. A true, unbiased opinion will be hard to come by between December 1st and the February signing date, so you may want to turn to this book as a friendly helper.

College coaches may or may not look favorably upon what the book has to say because I expose some of their favorite recruiting ploys. But I am not here to help the coaches. They already know the ropes. It is their business—something that you must remember all along. College coaches must do whatever is necessary to recruit well to ensure the success of future teams. The pressure to out-recruit the opponent has led to many problems. I hope the book will help **you** in making the best possible decision and I hope that it will educate you about matters which you will soon be dealing with.

One last word before I start: In no way do I profess to be a recruiting expert. I am simply someone who has been in your shoes and I understand what you are about to go through, so read on!

Chuck Mooney

1

TO THE ATHLETE

Congratulations! You are undoubtedly a fine athlete and a good football player, or you wouldn't even be reading this book. Finally, after all the hot practices, bumps, bruises, and lost blood, you have reached your goal...a chance to play college football, and maybe even a shot at an athletic scholarship. This scholarship is what you have worked so hard for all these years, right? You could receive five years of free education, free meals, free books, as well as free housing. Free, free, free. It sounds really nice doesn't it? Don't feel bad, you have definitely earned it, and don't let anybody tell you otherwise. Depending on what school you choose, you

The Recruiting Survival Guide

have probably saved your parents anywhere from ten to fifty thousand dollars. Nobody can argue that this is not a great accomplishment. Believe me, your parents sure will be thankful.

You are about to enter one of the most exciting times in your life, and I'll say this more than once: Relax and enjoy it. Don't let it consume you; it will if you let it. You may have the chance to meet some of the greatest coaches in America today, and the opportunity to tour some of the most beautiful and prestigious schools in the country. This is the chance of a lifetime. Never again in your life will people treat you this kindly, so milk it for all it's worth. At no time be intimidated. Ask as many questions as you feel necessary, and get answers. You are the boss. Remember that it is important to look out for number one.

More than likely you have been receiving mail since the end of your junior year. This is the time when most schools begin to make early contact with the "projected" top players around the country. Early on you can begin to formulate a basic idea of which schools you are most interested in. Let's say that you are contacted by thirty schools during the summer and some during your senior season. You should start now at least to consider which five schools you may wish to officially visit after the Christmas holiday. It will be in your best interest to eliminate immediately any schools that you are not interested in. Reduce the size of your list whenever possible.

On an official visit, the NCAA allows a college to cover all expenses necessary for you to visit its campus. The school will cover every cost from the minute you leave your house on Friday until you return home on Sunday afternoon. Transportation, meals, entertainment, and lodging are included in these costs. You may remain on the campus for forty-eight hours, so a school has two days to cram in as much information and fun as is humanly possible in that time period. It all sounds like great fun, and it really is, but remember: This is probably the biggest decision that you have yet to make in your life, so the more that you can learn about a school, the easier your final decision will be later on down the road.

The Recruiting Survival Guide

2

TO THE PARENTS

Regardless of whether you realize it or not, you deserve some credit too. You have obviously "done a fine job of raising your son." If that doesn't sink in right away, don't worry. You will have plenty of chances to hear that particular phrase in the next few months. During a coach's visit in your home, he will undoubtedly laud your son with so many compliments that you will find yourself asking if perhaps there has been a mistake, and if he is in the wrong house. Surely he can't be talking about your son. Believe me, my mom asked herself the very same questions. By the compliments

The Recruiting Survival Guide

your child will receive, you'll think you've raised the next savior of the world. Do not get "snowjobbed." He is still the same kid who won't eat his lima beans.

For those who have done the in-home visit before, you already know what to expect. But for our first-timers, in a nutshell, it's just a nice visit in your home. Initially, you will be visited by an assistant coach who has been recruiting your son. Later, if a school is serious about your son, the assistant will return accompanied by the head coach. It is simply an opportunity for the parents to meet the coaches and the coaches to get a look and feel of a player's home life. Much can be learned about a young man by examining his home life and his relationship with his family. Parents, be prepared to ask some questions. That is what this time is for. Some of the most commonly asked questions are the following:

1) **WHERE WILL MY SON LIVE?**
Living arrangements are something that will most definitely be talked about. On-campus housing will be provided free of charge, assuming your son receives a full athletic scholarship. Your son will live either in an athletic dormitory or in a mixed dorm shared by players and regular students alike. Please note that athlete-only dorms are to be phased out by 1996 according to new NCAA regulations. There are pros and cons to each set-up. The strictly-athletic dorms have been outlawed for numerous reasons. While some claim that they promote team unity, others say that they cause the athlete to be alienated from the general student

body. Some schools will allow players to live off-campus in homes or apartments and pay for them in amounts previously approved by the NCAA. Different coaches will have different opinions pertaining to living arrangements. No matter which system is used by a school, you can be assured of acceptable accommodations for your son.

2) **WHAT EXACTLY IS A SCHOLARSHIP?**

A scholarship is a five-year grant-in-aid which will cover the cost of books, fees, tuition, and room and board for your child. The scholarship is made up of five one-year financial grant-in-aids, one of which will be signed each year that your son remains in school. The only way for your son to lose his scholarship is to quit the team, get into some sort of legal trouble, or fail out of school.

3) **IF MY SON IS INJURED, DOES THE SCHOLARSHIP CONTINUE?**

With most coaches around the country, the answer is yes. The minute that your son makes a verbal commitment to a school, the university makes a similar commitment right back to him. However, it is the signed scholarship agreement that is legally binding. But, if your son called a coach and made a **verbal** commitment to attend his school, hung up the phone, walked out the front door, got hit by a truck, and was unable to play college ball, his scholarship would most likely still exist.

The Recruiting Survival Guide

If a player suffers a career-ending injury once in school, the school can place him on a medical exception list. This allows the school to keep the player on scholarship without counting against that school's number of eligible players. While the head coach is in your home, present this question to him. It may be interesting to see how he responds. No coach would yank a scholarship out from under an injured player. Other competing coaches would be all too willing to use such information against him in future recruiting wars.

4) IS THE SCHOOL CURRENTLY UNDER NCAA INVESTIGATION?

Once in a while you can surprise a coach and probably your son by asking a very impressive question. If the school that you are meeting with has any links to NCAA sanctions or investigations, feel free to ask any questions that you may have concerning this important subject. Your child's future is at stake, so make sure that you are well-informed on any subjects that are bothering you. A coach should be up-front and honest about any possible allegations made against him or his school.

Parents, whether you like it or not, your opinions in this ordeal will play an important role in your son's decision. It is of the utmost importance that you tread softly when voicing your views. Too little advice will make him feel as if he's all alone in his decision, as if he has been deserted. But, at the opposite end of the spectrum, too much advice can often apply undue pressure, especially if you are in favor of a school that your son is not particularly fond of. I have even heard of some parents going to church twice on the Sunday before signing date to pray for a miraculous change of heart in their son to attend the school of their choice.

When I was going through the recruiting process, I knew all along that my parents had one school in mind. Unfortunately, it was not the school that I eventually decided on. Our differences of opinion didn't cause any major problems, but it did cause me to ask myself some unnecessary questions in those last few days before signing date. Just remember that the final decision must be that of the player. He is the one who is going to have to live with the decision for the next four or five years. If you feel he is making a major mistake by choosing a certain college, let him know. It is your right as a parent. But at the same time, let him know that no matter what his final choice is, you will stick with him and support him. That's the important thing. This is one time that your son really needs family support.

While your son is being recruited by various schools, I would advise you to keep a "parents score sheet" on each school. This is a chart to record scores of one to ten (ten being the best) of the five final schools in many different categories. I'll give you a better idea of the score sheet in Chapter 20. As signing day approaches, you and your son should sit down in a quiet room and compare score sheets. Talk to one another as to why you scored a certain school as you did.

Also be prepared to do some phone answering during the later stage of the game. After a while your son will grow completely fearful of a telephone ring. Try to

The Recruiting Survival Guide

make things easier on him by fielding calls for the last few weeks if he doesn't want to talk. Many of the bigger recruits are forced to make a small list of exactly who he does and does not want to talk to. I know it may make you feel a bit like a secretary, but it may save your son a great deal of grief.

As I mentioned earlier folks, your son has just saved you a large chunk of money, so count your lucky stars, and be ready to assume your responsibilities during the next few months.

Remember:
1) Be supportive.
2) Be active.
3) Ask any and all questions (there are no rude questions during recruiting).
4) You too, should sit back and enjoy the recruiting experience.

4

Your Recruiter

If you haven't already, you will soon meet the man primarily responsible for all of the mail you have been receiving and the many phone calls you have been getting since your junior year. You have seen his handwriting and his signature and have heard his voice over the phone many times, but because of NCAA regulations, you won't be legally allowed to meet him until after December 1st. You may have noticed him on your practice field scouting you, but even a casual hello before the first of December is frowned upon by the NCAA rules committee. Restricting any contact until the De-

The Recruiting Survival Guide

cember date is a good rule. It limits the "open season" on recruits to two and one half months, and it enables the athlete to keep his complete attention on his all-important senior season. It is a rule set up basically to protect the recruit.

I'll give you fair warning: After December 1st, watch out! When you walk into the coach's office on that day, be prepared to be bombarded by many assistant coaches or recruiters. If their school is fortunate enough to get your attention, you will most definitely be seeing quite a bit of these gentlemen. These recruiters are assistant coaches who have probably covered your area for quite some time. Recruiters are assigned geographically, from year to year, to enable them to recruit better. The NCAA will allow a recruiter, during the next two and a half months, to visit with you at school three times and at home three times. If a school is serious about recruiting you, your recruiter may be accompanied by the head coach on at least one of the home visits. This one is considered the most important visit.

You will find through your experiences that each recruiter has his own style. Some will come across as the strictly-business type, while others will talk to you just as if they were your old friend. A few will take a laid-back approach, while a few others will take the hard-sell, high-pressure salesman approach. Unfortunately, this last one is a successful tactic against a scared eighteen-year-old kid. Whatever you do, don't allow yourself to be pressured into committing to a visit that you do not want to take. This is your show, don't waste a visit by letting some sales whiz come in and scare you into seeing his school. Being from the state of Texas, I had the opportunity to be exposed to a lot of the hard-

Chuck Mooney

sell style of recruiting. In the world of recruiting, it is different strokes for different folks. If a coach appeals to you, check more into his school. Ask parents, high school coaches, and most importantly yourself, if his school is the type of school you could see yourself attending.

If these recruiters have the proper outlook, they can be very helpful in enabling you to formulate your decision. Of course, it is their job to tell you all the great things about their school, but a few good coaches will also give you honest information about other schools. Usually, the information that you get from a coach about another school will be truthful.

One thing that you will find particularly amazing is that the coaching ranks across the country are like a big family tree. By a family tree I mean that at one time everyone worked with someone else at another school, or at one time a coach may have played for another coach, or many other incredible combinations of relationships. It's really amazing. The reason I bring this up is to show you that most of these coaches are not going to bad-mouth one another.

I'm not saying that you're not going to run across some occasional negative recruiting. This occurs when a school tells you every bad thing that has ever happened to a certain school that you may have an interest in. You will hear anything from rumors of scandals to low graduation rates. Some coaches are not above this old fashioned mud-slinging. When and if you come across this type of recruiting, take it for exactly what it's worth. If you are told something so negative that it would possibly make you change your mind about a school, do yourself a favor and check it out with some-

The Recruiting Survival Guide

one who would know, like the coach who is being slandered. He will appreciate you giving him the chance to defend himself. Avoid pitting two coaches against one another. You may run into negative recruiting as the signing date nears because this is a time when emotions run highest. Much can be learned in the last couple of weeks about a coach because many coaches will reveal their true personality under the pressure of an ever approaching signing date.

One other trap that you can run into is looking at a school simply because you like their recruiter. That is one of the biggest mistakes that you can make, yet it often happens. I can use myself as a perfect example of what can occur. I had been receiving letters from a school since my junior year, but I really had no interest in them whatsoever. Sure enough, when December 1st rolled around there was a recruiter in the coach's office at school to speak with me. Boy, was he my kind of guy. I had a great chat with him and really enjoyed his company. Half-seriously, I told him that I would consider his school and told him to keep in touch.

As time went on I soon found myself entertaining thoughts of attending this school. I knew that it wasn't the school for me, but I liked the recruiter so much that I didn't have the heart to say no. Eventually, he caught on to what was going on in my head, mainly because I wouldn't commit to a visit. After he came out and asked me what my true feelings were, we had a long talk and I eventually had the guts to admit that the only reason I had started thinking about his school was because of the way I felt for him as a friend. As much as he wanted to tell me to keep thinking of his school, he leveled with me and said that I should not visit a school simply because of an assistant coach.

An assistant coach should be the first to admit that he doesn't plan on being an assistant forever. Coaching is a business like any other business. There are promotions to coordinator and head coaching jobs that any assistant someday hopes for. Even coaches climb the corporate ladder. Needless to say, that assistant coach remained my good friend and we stayed in touch throughout the time before my decision. Telling him the truth hurt a little bit, but it just wouldn't have been fair to keep dragging him along when I knew that I had no true interest in his school.

Not only are these recruiters around to recruit you to their respective schools, but the good ones will also help you out if you need questions answered or an honest opinion regarding another school. Take advantage of their knowledge and learn from what they say and how they act. Enjoy these coaches and get comfortable around them. You will be seeing quite a bit of them for a while.

The Recruiting Survival Guide

4

THE HEAD COACH

One of the greatest thrills of the entire recruiting affair is having the chance to meet some of the most successful head coaches in the country. You may have seen these men on television every week, on magazine covers, or in the newspapers for as long as you have been following college football. And now the fact that you may have these very same men in your home, possibly eating at your dinner table, is a little intimidating in itself. What do I wear? How do I act? What if I don't know what to say to him? These and many other questions may be running through your head prior to a famous head coach's visit. My advice to you would be

The Recruiting Survival Guide

not to worry. These coaches are just like anybody else. They will be all fun and games because they don't face as many of the pressures of recruiting. The assistant coaches do all the dirty work. The head coach simply makes an appearance for posterity. His visit is mainly a chance for mom and dad to get to know him personally. Nine out of ten times if your parents prefer one particular coach, his school will be the one that they will prefer too.

Every coach will have unique personality traits. Meeting with a successful head coach is almost like magic because you know that you are speaking with a potential legend. In my experience, I had the opportunity to meet some of the finest coaches in the country.

Ex-Michigan head man, Bo Schembechler, now in the Detroit Tigers front office, had to be one of the most colorful characters to ever coach football. The man was truly a delight. Bo could tell a story and put away a good, hearty meal with the best of them. The night he ate dinner in my home I sat completely mesmerized by the tales he told. I hold few to be greater than this man in the collegiate coaching ranks. He did great things for Michigan and college football.

Another great Big Ten coach that I had the pleasure of meeting was Ohio State's Earle Bruce, who is now building a strong program at Colorado State. Coach Bruce is a believer in strong tradition, and what better place for tradition than at Ohio State? Coach Bruce is the type of guy who talks to you on your own level. He would talk to me and not at me. I will never forget his home visit which happened to be on Super Bowl Sunday. I honestly believe he is one of few coaches in the country who could have come into a recruit's home on the day of the Super Bowl and still have a successful visit. We had a great time watching the game and talking about Ohio State during commercials and half time. At no time did he feel like he had to compete with the television. He was content just to sit with my family and watch the game. That's the kind of guy he is.

Bill McCartney of the University of Colorado is as good and honest a man as I ever hope to meet. He is a strong Christian whose deep religious strength is a great asset to his Colorado teams. I deeply respect him for the excellent rebuilding job he has done at Colorado. He has brought back national powerhouse status to a squad that had been all but destroyed by previous coaching staffs. However, I was personally disappointed to see Coach Mac pass up the opportunity to set a modern-day precedent for honesty when he failed to reverse the outcome of the controversial "5th Down" play in a 1990 win over Missouri.

One of the few coaches that I can even put in the same league with Bo Schembechler as a people person is the coach who eventually signed me, Jim Wacker, of Texas Christian University. Jim Wacker has a personality unlike any I've ever encountered before. His enthusiasm for the game and refreshing zest for life were enough to make me believe that T.C.U. was the place for me. As I told a few local papers, attesting to his persuasive, confident attitude, "I have the feeling that Coach Wacker could sell screen windows to a submarine commander." He is also a man who preaches a hard line on cleaning up college athletics, a stance that made him unpopular with some in the coaching ranks. His past actions prove his sincerity on the matter. If you like a positive mental attitude and fired-up

The Recruiting Survival Guide

"smashmouth" football, then Jim Wacker is your man.

Remember these few things: Do not ever be intimidated by these guys. They are just like your recruiters, only ten or twenty years later on in their careers. Enjoy every minute that you spend with the head coach, and don't be so awe-struck that you can't ask questions. Just think, some of these coaches may be destined for the Hall of Fame, so meeting them may be something to tell your grandchildren about someday.

5

GET A CALENDAR

Before you get into the full swing of things, I would suggest that you purchase two small calendars with spaces big enough to keep notes on. Keep one by the phone and one in your room. Record reserved dates for a coach's visit and the dates that you plan on visiting schools. Without serious organization, the next two and a half months could be very hectic. Imagine the horror of scheduling visits with two different schools on the same weekend! Keep up with what is going on and keep it written down on your calendar.

The Recruiting Survival Guide

6

Discerning Truth From Flattery

Through the next few months you are going to meet a lot of people and you are going to hear a lot of nice things about yourself. You need to be sharp enough to be able to know the difference between sincere truth and simple recruiting talk.

When speaking to a college coach, never let yourself be told that he can make you a star in the National Football League. Any time a coach mentions the N.F.L., you should become a bit cautious. Some recruits will let themselves be lured to a school by promises of future

The Recruiting Survival Guide

fame and fortune in pro football. But let me tell you that any coach who promises that he can put you in the pros is either lying to you or trying to look through a crystal ball. Let's be reasonable, your chances of being struck by lightning are greater than making the N.F.L. Sure you know that you are good, and someday maybe you will make it to the pros, but for now you haven't even played one down of major college football. There's no way a coach can predict future N.F.L. stardom.

Keep in mind that you may be the top-dog now, but wherever you eventually sign you will be surrounded by players as good, if not better than you. No matter how big and bad you are there is always going to be someone bigger and badder around the next corner. Don't allow a coach's flattery go to your head.

Also take in stride coaches who have visions of you making All-American. Nothing can be decided until you step on that field. Some coaches may have optimistic visions of your future, but ask him just exactly how many recruits he has said the same thing to. Just be realistic and honest with yourself through it all.

The same goes for promises of a starting position the minute you walk on campus. I don't care how good a high school player you were, high school and college are two different worlds, as you will find out as soon as you report for two-a-days in August. Two things should enter your mind if a coach tries to promise you a starting job sight unseen. First, how fair is that to the guy who is the starter right now? He has worked hard to earn his position. How fair is it to give his job to an untested high school senior? Second, put yourself in his shoes two years from now. How would you feel if you were the projected starter and you knew that a recruiter was out on the streets promising your starting job to a recruit? You would be hurt and deservedly upset. Believe me, sometimes anything will be said to win a recruit's favor. Your day will come and you will get more than a fair shot to <u>earn</u> that starting position.

The Recruiting Survival Guide

Chuck Mooney

7

THE RATING SERVICES

Around the country there are many publications known as ratings services. These publications rate high school football players both regionally and nationally and are headed up by what are known as "superscouts." One man considered to be one of the foremost "superscouts" is Max Emfinger, who is based in Houston, Texas. Scouts like Max go nationwide to study a player's statistics, both on and off the field. They study such vital statistics as height, weight, 40-yard dash speed, grade point average and last but not least, any

The Recruiting Survival Guide

extra-curricular activities outside of football.

After this pertinent information is accumulated, the "superscout" feeds the data into his trusty computer and out comes what is known as a player's rating. The point scale is usually set up with a score of one-hundred being the best. When the scout compiles all the players who he feels are the tops at their positions, he will break them into subgroups, such as All-American and All-Region teams. The aim of the superscout and his rating service is to inform colleges of players all over the country who they may not get the chance to see play personally.

Several national publications annually choose their own All-American squads, the most highly touted of these being the <u>Parade</u> All-American team and the <u>U.S.A. Today</u> team. Local papers will also run several All-District, Area, and State teams after the completion of a season. Some states even have what is known as a "Blue-Chip" list or a "Super-Sixty" list. All are chosen by coaches or sports writers.

Basically what all these honorable lists amount to is good publicity. It is a great thrill to see your name in print in the Sunday morning paper or in a newsletter, but if you come out and ask most colleges, they don't put too much stock in what the ratings services have to say. They are helpful in exposing programs to players in another region who they may not have an opportunity to see play, but their word is not always the Gospel truth. They are forecasts, simply predictions based on a player's potential. Every year since 1966, <u>Parade</u> magazine has published their highly touted team. Interestingly enough, in the 1985 Heisman Trophy balloting, not one of the top 10 vote receivers was a <u>Parade</u>

All-American and the two quarterbacks from that 1985 <u>Parade</u> team never rose to the top of the college teams that they signed with. So don't give up hope if your name doesn't appear on each and every list in town. An awful lot of politics exists behind the scenes in regards to picking the All-This-and-That teams. If your name hasn't been included on a list, just be patient. Nothing is ever proven off of the football field, and newspaper clippings have never won a game.

For those of you who have been fortunate enough to have your names included on a few lists, a big congratulations to you. You can be proud of what you have accomplished. A great many outstanding players have never made these lists and you have. One word of advice: Please save every press clipping with your name in it for the future. I suggest even starting a scrapbook. After talking with many ex-college athletes, those that saved clippings and articles were glad, and those that threw everything out wished that they could go back and save all their memorabilia. Trust me, someday it will be fun to drag out your old recruiting clippings and reminisce with your kids or grandchildren.

The main thing that I wish to stress in this chapter is that your collegiate career doesn't necessarily ride on the opinion of one man's publication or one reporter's All-State team. Publicity is great but it doesn't win ball games. Keep that in mind.

The Recruiting Survival Guide

8

ILLEGAL RECRUITING

There is a possibility that sometime during your recruitment you will be approached with some rather lucrative proposals aimed at luring you to a certain college. You may be offered money or something else of value. Most often those making the offers will be the infamous overzealous alumni, but it also could be coming straight from the coaching staff themselves, although NCAA crackdowns have cut down on the latter. In most cases the alumnus is going against a staff's wishes when he engages in dirty recruiting, but some people will stop at nothing.

If you are ever approached with any suspicious of-

The Recruiting Survival Guide

fers there should be no question in your mind as to what to do. There is a right decision and a wrong decision. You must decline the offer no matter how tempting it may be, because once you accept just one offer there is no turning back. The minute you are on the take (a receiver of money), you are marked for life. One payoff is more than enough to ruin your whole life. In the past, only the school was punished for illegal dealings, but those times have changed. The athlete as well as the payoff man is thought to be guilty.

Is the money you may receive worth jeopardizing your career? That is a question that you must answer yourself. When you take the money you are putting your future on the line. You are not the only one affected either. Besides directly harming yourself, you hurt your entire family, your coaches, your teammates, and your school, as well as college athletics across the country.

Only certain recruits will be targets of illegal recruiting inducements. A college coach told me that most alumni feel that poor minority players are more apt to take illegal offers. If someone offers you money you may feel that he really likes you, quite frankly, it is quite the opposite. If someone offers you money they are directly insulting you, your morals, and your intelligence. They are jeopardizing your career by offering you payoffs. They obviously have no respect for you or your future. Don't be a chump and allow yourself to be bought! If you come across as an intelligent, assertive, classy guy, then you won't have to worry about being approached by any sleazy offers. A mature recruit is too much of a risk to approach with a bribe, for fear that he may blow the whistle on a school's neat little operation.

Just because you are a good athlete does not give you the right to receive special illegal payoffs. Isn't the opportunity to get a free education enough?

If you are approached and have any doubt about whether to take the money or not, just look inside yourself and dig up a little self-respect. You don't need any hand-outs. There are no shortcuts in life. The only rewards in life that are truly sweet are the ones you earn, not the ones handed to you on a silver platter.

Any spending money that you may need during the year can be easily made with a summer job, found by the school if necessary. If you do get a job found by the school, make sure that it is a legitimate job. No twenty dollars an hour for turning on the stadium lights. Don't sell yourself short.

Coach Jim Wacker of Texas Christian University is one coach who is a strong believer in the importance of cleaning up college athletics. When he arrived at T.C.U. by way of Southwest Texas State, he soon sent out a letter to just about every major college coach in America, pleading with his fellow coaches to help him eliminate the illegal actions. This letter caused him to be ridiculed by most every coach that received it. Most denied that there was actually a problem in recruiting.

A few prominent coaches did echo Wacker's concerns and their efforts continued. For years the NCAA has been asking schools to aid in the clean-up effort by "self-policing"– to come forward and report any underhanded dealings rather than sweep them under the rug. In the early stages of the 1985 season, it was discovered by a member of Jim Wacker's staff that seven of T.C.U.'s best players were on the take. Coach Wacker had to

The Recruiting Survival Guide

follow through with what he had been preaching all along. He was forced to dismiss the seven players from the team. Unfortunately, T.C.U. was still dealt a severe punishment including loss of television coverage and some scholarships. The only thing this resulted in was the assurance that no team will ever blow the whistle on themselves again.

One of the seven players dismissed was pre-season Heisman Trophy favorite, Kenneth Davis. In a period of five days Kenneth went from football hero to the center of an ugly recruiting scandal. The following is an excerpt from an interview with Kenneth Davis by <u>Fort Worth Star-Telegram</u> writer, Mike Jones.

> "The biggest thing I would tell an 18-year-old is that the money they are offering you is not worth the rewards you are going to receive mentally and morally and the way people are going to respond to you. The money was there...and I took it. That's the biggest reason I took it. Because it was there. But I was wrong," he said, "I was wrong to the extent that every dream in my life that I've had has been thrown away because I was offered money from an alumni and I took it. I would tell someone that the greatest thing about going to a university is to get your degree, be your own man and don't let somebody entice you. Live to your own standards and what you believe in. I've thrown it all away. I threw it away when was 18 years old."

Chuck Mooney

Kenneth has since found a place in the National Football League as a member of the 1991 Buffalo Bills Super Bowl team. Although he has overcome the scandal of 1985, I think that Kenneth would probably admit that despite his current success, a piece is still missing that can never be put into place. I think we can all learn something from Kenneth Davis' mistake.

What it all boils down to is your ability to deny the temptation and discern right from wrong. It's up to each of you to make your own personal decision. Say yes and you will be putting it all on the line. Say no and you will be taking your first steps toward a great future, no matter which school you choose.

The Recruiting Survival Guide

9

THE VISIT

In your decision process you will have to narrow down your list to just five schools. The NCAA allows only five expense-paid campus visits per athlete. You may say to yourself, "Only five!", but let me tell you, if you do take all five visits, after that fifth and final one, you will be mentally, physically, and emotionally exhausted. In my opinion you should need only three visits, but if you feel that five are necessary then take all five. After Christmas, schools will be ready for you to commit to a campus visit. Your recruiter has more than likely been mentioning this since the first time the two of you met. Your visit is the first step toward his get-

The Recruiting Survival Guide

ting you to sign with his school. He knows that if you don't think enough of a school to visit it, then you definitely won't be thinking of attending there next year. If a coach gets you to commit to an on-campus visit then he has won the first part of the battle. The after-Christmas rush is when it all happens. Up to that point you may be able to stall schools by telling them you will make a decision as to which schools you want to visit over your Christmas vacation, but be prepared to reveal to the recruiters your final visitation choices after Christmas vacation at the latest. Once you've told your recruiters which schools you plan to visit the hard part is over. Now prepare to do some serious evaluating. The next four or five weekends will be some of the most important of your life.

WHAT TO PACK?

You may think that you are old enough to decide what to take on a weekend trip, and you are absolutely correct. However, here are some pointers:

1) Parents: An excellent Christmas gift is one of the big, flexible, travelling duffle bags for your jet-set, scholarship-bound son. They range in price from $15-$75 dollars for a decent bag. They are more than worth the investment because they are easier to handle than a hard suitcase. Furthermore, in large airports like Houston or Atlanta, a shoulder strap comes in handy. They are also much easier to cram into the ever-shrinking overhead storage compartments in airplanes.

2) Recruits: Don't put off packing until the last minute. Thursday night at midnight is not a good time to start the chore of packing if you're leaving Friday afternoon. Early in the week, make sure all of the clothes that you'd like to pack are clean. Mom doesn't enjoy getting out of bed to do your wash at midnight. I know for a fact that such requests are rather upsetting for moms. In order for you to have a completely positive attitude about your upcoming trip you'll need to get all packing done before Thursday night.

3) What type of clothes you pack depends entirely upon the climate of the school you plan to visit. If you visit a Big Ten school pack your sweaters and a coat. Keep in mind that if you're visiting a Northern school, chances are that in January and early February it's bound to be pretty cold outside. Call your recruiting coach or recruiting coordinator for a weather report. Also ask if there will be a need for a sportscoat and a tie. Most schools don't ask you to worry about this but a few schools present a fancy dinner on Saturday night and they like to see you looking good. All in all, don't dress like a slob. Look nice, but it is also important to be comfortable as well.

4) Pack a good, comfortable pair of walking shoes. You will find that you will be doing quite a bit of walking all day Saturday so try to avoid painful blisters.

5) Remember to pack the bare necessities, such as deodorant, toothbrush, and clean under-

The Recruiting Survival Guide

wear. Asking to borrow, or needing to purchase these items can sometimes be a bit embarrassing in your new surroundings.

6) Depending on where you plan to visit, I would suggest that you pack a camera, especially if you will be visiting somewhere you have never been before.

7) If you live in a warm, Southern climate and plan to visit a Northern school in a cold climate, you will need a warm jacket. Sometimes the only jacket you own is your high school letter jacket. Before my visits I was given a bad piece of advice. I was advised not to wear my letter jacket because I might receive some ribbing from students for being a recruit. Nonsense! I wish now that I had not gone out and spent my good money on a jacket I will never wear again. Go ahead and wear your letter jacket. You worked to earn it. Be proud and ignore any possible sort of college-man ribbing that you may receive.

Virtually every visit will be a good one but some will be better than others for different reasons. Each school will have something different to offer. You must decide which school appeals to you the most. When talking with other recruits you may find that you have totally differing opinions about your visit. Sometimes it seems as if you are talking about two different schools, but don't let this sway your opinion.

Going into my first weekend visit, I had absolutely no idea what to anticipate in the next two days, so I've prepared for you an outline of a basic visit.

Chuck Mooney

1) You will leave sometime Friday afternoon and fly to the respective school, arriving between 4:00 and 7:00 p.m. The school will pay for the airline ticket which you will receive either from

The Recruiting Survival Guide

the coach himself, at the ticket counter, or through the mail. If you need a ride to the airport the school will pay for a cab or pay for the cost of gas to the airport. Make sure that you accurately log all mileage or keep receipts for proper reimbursement.

2) When you land at your destination you will be greeted either by your recruiter or some other member of the coaching staff. He will take you to your hotel and give you a chance to freshen up and unpack. All recruits are housed in deluxe accommodations at a local hotel, which is also paid for by the university.

3) After you get a chance to rest, you are off to a fancy dinner with your recruiting coach and possibly other recruits. You are encouraged to eat until you can't eat another bite. The food is always delicious and plentiful. Don't be shy about eating a lot of food; coaches love big eaters. You can expect to leave your visit about ten pounds heavier.

4) After dinner the coaches will set you free with a prearranged host. This host is a football player, usually a redshirted freshman or sophomore, although some programs prefer that you are led around by established name-players. This host is usually set up with your personality type in mind. Coaches definitely research this subject closely because so much of your decision is based on your weekend visit. If you are basically a quiet guy, a school is not going to set you up with a party animal for the weekend. Your host will take you out on the town,

more than likely with other host-and-recruit pairs. You may stop in clubs or restaurants or an occasional party at a frat house. Some guys like to just go see a movie, or cruise a local mall. This is all meant to give you a chance to meet the players and students of the school in their natural environment, away from football. Remember that you're not going to attend classes with just football players, so welcome the chance to meet other people too. If you choose to sign with this school, you will be spending the next four or five years of your life with these people, so make sure that you fit in. One very important thing to remember is that if you are not a drinking man do not feel like you have to drink. Most often, if you are not a partier, your host won't be either. Be yourself and act however you are the most comfortable.

5) After this night out on the town, your host will take you back to your room where you will grab a couple hours of shut-eye before your big day on Saturday. Depending on the program, you will either be sharing a room with your host or a fellow recruit. The next morning you will rise all too early and eat a huge breakfast. Then your big day will begin.

6) All day Saturday you will be bombarded with academic meetings and other fun-filled get togethers with counselors, professors, and department deans. The only bad thing about academic meetings is that all you have on your mind is getting some sleep, but this is a great time to find out important academic informa-

The Recruiting Survival Guide

tion. You will also discover one hundred new ways to keep from yawning in someone's face while he or she is talking to you.

7) During the day you will have an opportunity to meet personally with both your position coach and the head coach. These meetings are always great because, as I said before, it is a thrill to meet some of these famous coaches. At this point you may begin to learn in detail where the school sees you fitting into their program.

8) At some point during the day there will be time allotted for fun. This time could be spent doing anything from attending a basketball or hockey game to taking a tour of the town or enjoying the nearby scenery. Recruits always look forward to these side trips because they offer an excellent chance for you to get off your feet and relax, sometimes even sleep.

9) Saturday night you will be fed a big dinner, as usual, and then entertained with another big night on the town. Expect even less sleep than you got the previous night.

10) Sunday morning you will wake up feeling something like a zombie. After another huge breakfast you'll have a final farewell chat with the head and position coaches. The chat with the head coach is always interesting because it is the coach's chance to leave you with some valuable piece of advice which he hopes will sway your opinion to his school. I would advise against getting caught up in the emotion of the moment. Some coaches will try to get

you to commit on the spot. Why not wait and think it over and talk to your parents before making a commitment?
11) Sometime before you leave, whether it be on Saturday or Sunday, you will get a quick look at the facilities and the stadium. Be sure to ask to see a dorm room, or any other type of athletic housing. You'll need to see where you may be living for the next four or five years.
12) Now it's off to the airport, which offers another chance to get some more sleep. Once again, the school will cover transportation costs from the airport to your home. If you are not given money to get home, be sure to ask a coach before you leave. Specify what the money is for and do not take a penny more than it will cost to get home.

The actual visit is usually what makes a recruit's decision. Do not base a decision on whether you meet a nice girl at a school or not. You can find pretty girls at any school, so don't let any factors as trivial as that enter into your considerations.

Be inquisitive on your visit. Ask your host any questions. When asked, hosts will generally give you surprisingly honest answers.

During your academic appointments discuss possible majors. If you are like most high school seniors, you have little or no idea as to what you want to do with your life. Even if you do have a pretty good idea about what you want to major in, don't neglect other options because the average college student will switch his or her major at least once. You will not have to officially

The Recruiting Survival Guide

declare a major until the end of your sophomore year, but an early decision can give you a good start toward an on-time graduation. If you do have a specific interest, ask whether a school has a good department in that field. Inquire about suggested course loads and the semester hour credit system. To most high school seniors, the credit system of a college makes no sense whatsoever. Ask also about the athletic tutorial program and academic counselors. With the new NCAA rulings concerning academic standards, more and more emphasis is being placed on education, as it should be. Let's not lose sight of why you're going to school in the first place.

Besides the five official visits, a recruit may take an unofficial visit to a school. This is a visit by a recruit to a campus by his own free will and at his own expense. If you live near some schools that you are interested in, the summer before your senior year is an excellent time to get a good look at campuses and meet with coaches. This is legal, and college coaches encourage it.

For you moms and dads who are wondering, you **are** allowed to attend the visits with your sons. There is only one catch – you must cover your own expenses. If you wish to do this, contact your recruiting coach and he will take care of all the particulars for you.

Relax, enjoy your visits, ask questions, and have fun!

10

STEROIDS

While you are on your visit you will learn quite a bit about the players on the team. Some of what you learn will be good and some not so good. One thing that you will encounter on any major college football team in the country is the use of anabolic steroids. Anabolic steroids are a testosterone drug which are used to enhance an athlete's physical performance. Proper usage of the drug can double upper and lower body strength and dramatically increase speed and endurance. Through the right channels it can easily be obtained by anyone wishing to do so. Virtually every college interior lineman has had some form of contact with steroids. The pressure to succeed on the college and pro level is tre-

The Recruiting Survival Guide

mendous, and the success rate of steroids, with proper use, is enticing. With these two factors in mind, it's no small wonder that the use of steroids is so widespread.

But I must warn you: What sounds like magic can end up a nightmare. The drawbacks of the wonder drug far outweigh the positive aspects. Regular use or eventual abuse can lead to heart, liver, and kidney failure, irritability, crankiness, and a reduced sex drive due to

Chuck Mooney

testicular atrophy. The list of side-effects is endless, but players under pressure to be the best succumb to pressure from other players and coaches every year. The emphasis to win at any cost becomes so profound that many of these players eventually resort to steroids.

The majority of high school players have already been exposed to "roids," either by using them or by knowing someone who has. The public is not as ignorant on

The Recruiting Survival Guide

the subject as they once were. The choice is yours, but in my opinion, the dangers outweigh the rewards.

If you are even considering using steroids then I beg you to research the subject; find out what you will be pumping into your body and what risks you will be taking. An excellent series of facts and testimonials can be found in the May 1, 1985 issue of <u>Sports Illustrated</u>. It is an in-depth look at steroids, the pros and cons, and a true account of how "juice" almost ended the life of N.F.L. lineman, Steve Courson. Other more recent articles can be found in <u>Sports Illustrated</u> as well. The February 20, 1989 issue contains the tragic story of the steroid-related death of a high school athlete. And in the October 24, 1988 issue, former South Carolina lineman Tommy Chaikin tells of his steroid nightmare. I urge you to go to your local library and read these articles.

Chuck Mooney

11

TAKING CARE OF THE HOMEFRONT

During this new and exiting time in your life, it is easy to lose sight of important matters at home. Grades, friends, family, and even your senior football season can take a back seat to the new wave of attention and popularity you will gain.

Most high school coaches will wisely hold a player's mail through the duration of their senior season and not allow much contact by colleges during the season

The Recruiting Survival Guide

for the simple reason that too many players around the country every year aren't ready to handle the limelight. A player needs to keep his mind on the task at hand. It is all too easy to start looking to the future. I have seen some great high school talents fall victim to the "big-head syndrome," and in the process, go out and have a terrible senior season. Believe me, a coach's opinion about you can change overnight if he sees that you have blown off your final high school season. Work hard up until the very last day of high school. Do not slack off. Set your goals high and make your last year of high school football one which you'll never forget.

One thing that you'll have to face during the season is having college scouts attending your games. Now for some players, knowing that a scout is up in the stands watching him play is enough to make him want to die. What you need to do is just go out and forget that anybody important is up in the stands and play the type of game that you are capable of playing. If you do have a bad game when a scout is in attendance, don't worry. A good coach is not going to base his opinion of your talent on just one game, so it's not the end of the world.

Most importantly, don't let your studies at school slide. Now that you are a jet-set celebrity it is dangerously easy to fall behind in the classroom. Do not let yourself fall into that trap! Be absolutely sure to keep up with the work assigned. If you know a college visitation is going to cause you to miss a day of school, get your assignments early and do extra work. Explain to your teachers ahead of time what you are doing for the next few months. Most of them will understand if your work should happen to slide, and try to help you main-

Chuck Mooney

tain good grades. There is no worse feeling than getting bogged down with a backup of school work when you are trying to decide where you want to go to college.

While you are going through the recruiting process, enjoy, but also keep up with obligations on the homefront.

The Recruiting Survival Guide

12

ALUMNI

Just like anything else in this world, there are good and bad within any group of people. The same holds true with college alumni. Alumni are basically active graduates of a particular school. The ones that you will come into contact with may be particularly fond of a given sport or department of their alma mater. Football alumni are a formidable bunch. Without active positive alumni support, sporting programs would be non-existent. They are definitely an important part of intercollegiate athletics. Unfortunately, some try to play

The Recruiting Survival Guide

too large a role in luring a recruit to his or her school. Sometimes alumni must be taken with a grain of salt.

Alumni can be found in every city representing any school across the country. Schools sometimes notify local alumni that there is a prospect in their area, or alumni may become aware of your interest in their alma mater through the local sports page.

Often they are asked to make a friendly phone call just to let you know that they're interested in you and hoping that you will consider their university. It is the few alumni who make it solely their responsibility to get you to their school that become a problem. They just want to be able to say, "I got this guy to my school!" or "That's my boy!"

Some nights the last thing that you need is for some overzealous alumnus to call you at home to chat when you've been on the phone all night with every coach in the country. All you need to do is politely ask him or her to allow you to do your homework or to go to bed. If he or she persists, politely excuse yourself and hang up.

Some alumni take it upon themselves to win a recruit's favor with financial inducements. I'm talking about illegal recruiting. If you are ever approached by any type of suspicious offer, flat out tell the alumni to back off. If the offers should persist, notify the school that is being represented.

Times are changing, and as I said earlier, no longer is just the alumnus or the school going to be punished. The athlete is now included in the penalty. Coaches, along with the NCAA, are calling for a self-induced clean-up of the collegiate athletic system. A coach won't allow illegalities to go on because of stiff sanctions being dealt to schools caught with their hand in the cookie jar. The coach who does allow payoffs to continue may be caught one day soon, and you don't want to be there with him when he does.

During the stretch prior to signing day, schools may bring out the "big guns" as far as alumni contacts are concerned. Some famous people may be contacting you to gain some ground for their alma mater. Professional athletes, celebrities and some political officials will call, write, or send you telegrams to help you along in your decision. Take these contacts in stride because you won't hear from most of these people ever again. Do not allow your opinion to be swayed by fancy alumni treatment.

Alumni are a great, helpful group of people, but the ones who go beyond the boundaries of right and wrong do nothing but abandon the best interest of you, the recruit.

The Recruiting Survival Guide

13

SUMMER JOBS

One of the privileges of becoming a member of a team is that your school may help you find a summer job. Most often the jobs will be high-paying ones that will leave you with enough energy to work out at the end of the day. A few years back, many schools would obtain jobs for their athletes that paid twenty dollars an hour and entailed sitting by the pool or turning the stadium lights on and off. With the recent NCAA investigations, universities are finally straightening up and doing things the right way. Take advantage of opportunities that your school may provide, but keep it on the level.

If your recruiter does not mention a summer job, feel

The Recruiting Survival Guide

free to ask if the school will be able to help with employment opportunities. It is not an obligation for them to help you out, and the coaches must first tend to upper-classmen already on the team. Summers are important because NCAA rules prohibit any scholarship athlete from earning an income during the school year, excluding official holidays like Christmas or spring break, so this is the primary time for you to earn your income. Rather than sitting around and watching cartoons all summer, it is important to make enough money to help get you through the school year.

One often-overlooked financial opportunity for full-scholarship athletes is the Pell Grant. Every year, the Federal Government gives away thousands of dollars in grants to the general student population. In past years, money given to scholarship athletes was restricted to certain amounts. However, these restrictions are no longer in effect and athletes are eligible to receive the full amount. Check with the financial aid department of the school you are planning to attend to see if you qualify for these Pell Grant funds.

Chuck Mooney

14

HANDLING THE PRESS

Whether you like it or not, you are now the subject of media coverage. The people want to know which college you will choose and it's the job of the press to keep the public informed. You are now in the public eye because you are newsworthy. And being newsworthy, anything you say or do will be held against you, as well as appear in the morning paper. Let me explain what I'm talking about.

The Recruiting Survival Guide

Every city has a newspaper. The size and style of this paper directly reflects the size of its city. Some towns, such as my hometown, Houston, has two major newspapers. Within most major newspaper sports departments, there is a reporter in charge of covering local high school sports action. This reporter has probably been covering various major ball games all year long and has his or her weekly section which wraps up the week's high school action. It is the job of this reporter to cover the three stages of a high school season. These three stages are: The regular season, the playoffs, and the recruiting season. It is the job of the high school sports editor, for the next three months, to feature charts and columns dedicated solely to high school football recruiting. It is also his or her job to be the first to know of your opinions so that his or her readers can be the first to know too. You can expect some stringers or the reporters themselves to make telephone contact with you frequently to keep up to date on your decision process. Some may even leave you their name and number and make you promise to contact them should you make a move, whether it be a commitment or a secret last-minute visit. These tidbits are choice items for the high school recruiting reporter.

Sometimes when dealing with the press, valuable lessons are learned the hard way. The most important lesson being that "the pen is mightier than the sword." The press is responsible for a majority of public opinion. People tend to believe what they read. When talking over the phone to a reporter, be on constant guard about every word that comes out of your mouth. If you say it, they'll print it! There is no such thing as a friendly, heart-to-heart chat with a reporter. I hate to generalize like that, but you are better off playing it safe.

Some reporters will set you up to believe that they are just providing a listening ear, just to get some information out of you. I learned this the hard way. One evening late in the recruiting season, I received a call from a reporter whom I had been talking to for the past several weeks. At this time I had narrowed my list of five schools down to a smaller list of two. Although I had my choices narrowed down, I hadn't had the chance (nor the courage) to notify the three schools to let them know that I had cut them from my list. The reporter and I talked casually for a couple of minutes, mainly about the decisions of other recruits who had signed earlier that day. Eventually I let it slip that I had narrowed my list to two schools. I told her the ones that I had ruled out and explained to her that I hadn't had a chance to notify them of my decision against them. She said that she understood and that she would keep quiet.

Well, I thought that would be the end of that conversation, but I found out later that I was wrong. The next morning in the school library a friend brought the sports page to my attention. To my surprise the headline shockingly revealed that I had reduced my list to two schools. I read on and found much of the previous evening's conversation in the article. I felt betrayed by that particular reporter. I dreaded going home later that day because I knew that there would be a phone message list at least a mile long. I was right. Every alumni, recruiter, and head coach of the schools I had axed were attempting to reach me wondering what the heck was going on. I was forced to make a lot of apologies and eat a lot of my words. I finally explained to everyone what was going on in my head, but I learned that it

The Recruiting Survival Guide

would have been much easier and smoother if I had told the three schools instead of them reading of my decision in the paper.

The press isn't all bad. Quite often a reporter will do a fantastic feature article on you. It's great to see your smiling face on Sunday morning's sports page. Special articles are definitely worth clipping and saving forever.

Don't let the press scare you to death. Learn to use the press as a tool, but be extremely cautious about what you say to reporters. Remember, it is their job to get the story first. So just be careful and be prepared to be held accountable for what you say.

Chuck Mooney

15

SAYING "NO"

No matter how long you try to put it off, the time will come when you'll have tell some schools that you have decided against them. In the recruiting race, there is only one winner. There are no ribbons for second place. That's just the way it is. You can only go to one school and when you decide which one it is, it's your duty to inform the others with a phone call.

As early as December, you will face the first time that you have to tell a recruiter no. Of all of the mail that you have been receiving through the year, only one-half to two-thirds of these schools will actually pursue you as an actual "recruitable player." The first job for a

The Recruiting Survival Guide

coach is to get you to commit to an on-campus visit.

Remember that you are allowed to take five visits, which is more than enough, but when you have around twenty-five schools asking for you to visit, that means that you will have to say no at least twenty times.

When recruiters come in, listen to what they have to say. Often a recruiter's attitude will reflect a school's style. With many schools, you will know ahead of time whether you would want to visit or not. If you've always been a UCLA fan, then I would suggest that you jump at the chance to visit there. But if you have always rooted against a school, chances are that you probably won't visit that particular one.

When the time comes to tell a recruiter no, you must remember that this is business for him. No matter how nice he is or how close the two of you have become, he has done the exact same thing for many years before you. I'm not saying his feelings for you are insincere, but he has been at this game a while, and your rejection will not be the first one he has ever had. If you know a school is out of the picture, it is best for both you and the recruiter to be honest about it. It will keep him from calling you and it will give him time, money and energy to spend on a recruit that may truly be interested in his school. Sure he will be disappointed, but he must move on to work for other players. Most coaches will respect your decision. The ones that give you a hard time aren't worth worrying about. They need to do a lot of growing up. Go on your chosen visits and prepare for the next difficult battle.

The last time you'll have to tell a coach no is when you actually make your final decision. These final five coaches will have the benefit of having spent an extra month and a half with you and your family, whether on the phone or in your house. By this time a good recruiter will know everything about you right down to your dog's name. The aim is to build a close relationship with you. This is what makes it harder to say no to them. You have spent more time with these guys, so it only makes sense that it is harder to tell your new friend that you have chosen another school over his.

The thing to do once you reach a decision is to call the "winner" with the good news, then promptly call the other four schools and notify them as well. Do not let them hear about your final decision through the grapevine! That is not fair to them. Simply thank them very much for their time and interest, but let them know you have chosen another school. As I said, they are bound to be disappointed but they'll surely wish you well and be on their way.

Some will make a desperate, last ditch effort to sway your opinion. My advice to you is this: No matter what you do, once you tell one school yes, try to stick with that decision. After you've told one school yes, a change of heart only causes problems. I am sure that you have all heard the old saying that your first instincts are usually correct.

The main thing to keep in mind when faced with saying no is that this is a business for a recruiter. He has been told no before. Don't worry too much about hurting anyone's feelings. No recruiter gets every kid that he is after.

The Recruiting Survival Guide

Chuck Mooney

16

SECOND LEVEL PLAYERS

When recruits begin to tell certain schools no, their decisions make way for thousands of talented but overlooked players across the country. These players are often just as good as the top recruits, but for one reason or another they were simply passed over or underestimated by scouts, recruiting services and newspapers. If you feel you are one of these players, here is one simple piece of advice: Hang tight and be patient. I know that at first it is hard to see friends and teammates

The Recruiting Survival Guide

receiving mail and getting all the attention of the scouts, but trust me, your time will come.

You may start receiving calls in the last part of the recruiting season, which would be early February. Many calls are also received after the national signing date. Now schools that have scholarships left over can comb the nation for a solid player who perhaps got left behind. Do not be picky or bitter. Take any opportunity that is put before you if you truly want to play college football. There is no disgrace in signing late. I've already tried to explain to you what publicity is worth, so take the scholarship if you are ever offered.

If the calls never do come, you are still not out of options. There is no shame in writing or calling certain schools that you may be interested in. A typed, personal letter expressing your interest and a listing of your vital statistics may open some doors for you. When contacting a school on your own to express your interest, be prepared to select and send two of your best game films. These will be helpful in a college's evaluation of you.

Schools may think enough of you to ask you to "walk-on" to their program. Walking-on simply means that you attend a school at your own cost and play football. If you prove your worth and impress the coaches, you may become eligible for a scholarship or financial aid the next year and the years after that. But you must be willing to foot the bill your freshman year. If you want to walk-on and need help securing funds to pay for your schooling I would suggest you consult <u>Barron's Complete College Financing Guide</u> (formerly <u>Barron's Dollars for Scholars</u>). This book is an excellent resource to help you tap into the vast number of scholarships and

Chuck Mooney

grants available.

Walk-ons are tough, determined, and love the game of football. My senior year at TCU, our Most Valuable Player was a guy who came in as a walk-on and eventually earned a scholarship. When he was in high school, all the scouts told him that he was too small to play Division I football. Walk-ons love proving their critics wrong.

Players with academic weaknesses that may have been ineligible for major college offers (Propostion 48 requires a minimum of 700 on the SAT or an 18 on the ACT for admission to a university) can also choose to go the junior college route. Even players who were overlooked because of lack of size or speed may opt for a couple of years of junior college to improve on their weaknesses. Major colleges recruit out of junior colleges every year. Often a large school will advise a recruit to attend a junior college with the intent of transferring him to the large school at the completion of his two year junior college stay.

It is these second level players that have the guts, determination and drive that often go on to star in the collegiate ranks. You could be one of them if the will is there!

The Recruiting Survival Guide

17

REDSHIRTING

You may have already heard the term "redshirt," or noticed that I have mentioned that a player may remain at a school for either four or five years. The way a player may stay in school for that extra year is by declaring one season a redshirt season.

The redshirt idea was formulated by the NCAA to aid both athletes and universities. The declaration of redshirt allows a player to play one extra year should he fall victim to a debilitating injury or if he doesn't have a chance to play his freshman year. In case of injury, a player may declare that season a redshirt season and use the remainder of the year to rehabilitate the

The Recruiting Survival Guide

injury rather than waste a year of eligibility. However, the most common use of the redshirt rule is in the case of an incoming freshman. The incoming freshmen who have no chance of playing during the season are usually redshirted.

The decision to redshirt is reached after a discussion with the head coach and the player. This year off enables the player to attend school for five years and still play in football games for four years.

You should know that in extreme circumstances a coach may be forced to play a freshman who has planned on redshirting. If you play just one down of one game (including post-season games) during the year, you forfeit that particular redshirt season. However, you have the option of declaring any of your remaining years as a redshirt season. Keep in mind that the redshirt rules are constantly being updated and changed. For unusual circumstances consult with your coach or athletic director.

During the redshirt season, a player goes through a regular practice along with the other varsity players. In practice, the redshirts may be used in the scout defenses and offenses and then be allowed to leave practice a few minutes early. They will be just like a regular member of the team except for the fact that they will not be active during the games on Saturday.

For incoming freshmen, the redshirt road is a normal one in an established program. Successful teams who recruit well year after year prefer to redshirt up to 95 percent of incoming freshmen. This procedure allows players to mature an extra year while lifting weights and strengthening their weaknesses. It is also a great opportunity to become very familiar with the mental aspect of the team's game plan.

Being redshirted leaves incoming freshmen with mixed emotions. The decision to redshirt will always be reached with the help of the head coach. He may suggest that a player wait a year to play but never will a coach redshirt a player against his will. The best argument that I have ever heard in favor of redshirting is this: Imagine being able to come back for one more year of high school football. As good as you may have been your senior year, an extra year could only make you better! It is only natural that this same situation would hold true with an extra year at the college level.

There is nothing dishonorable about being redshirted.

The Recruiting Survival Guide

It is something that must be thought about by both player and coach and decided upon together. Parents may also have a big say in this decision. It may be hard to get used to at first, but can be the best decision in many instances.

Redshirting also offers a great option academically. This way you will have a fifth year of free education in which to finish your degree, or if you have managed to graduate in four years, to work toward a master's degree. With a normal sixteen-hour semester courseload, it is possible to graduate in four years. And after football is over, a master's degree can be very handy to have on your resumé while job hunting.

Those of you who are fortunate enough to be in the right program at the right time may get the chance to come in and contribute early. But, for those of you who don't, the redshirt offers a great chance for you to get comfortable with your new surroundings and establish yourselves on the team before going into a game situation.

18

ACADEMICS

Do Not Skip This Chapter!!

I know that some of you are tired of hearing about the importance of academics, but you must remember the reason you're going to college in the first place... to learn! Football is merely a tool which helps us further our education and often gives us our only chance to do this for free. The following are some questions that you should get answers to while making your decision.

The Recruiting Survival Guide

1) CAN A COLLEGE ACCOMMODATE YOUR CHOSEN FIELD OF INTEREST?

If you have a pretty good idea of what you are interested in studying, ask what the school can offer you. If a school is particularly strong in a given area you will surely hear all about it, but at the same time a school should be honest and tell you if a department is weak in your chosen field.

2) ASK ABOUT CLASS SIZE.

Based on the size of the university and the type of class it is, class sizes may vary. No matter where you plan to attend you will run into some basic, required freshman courses that may have as many as five-hundred students in one class. You will hear horror stories of students waiting in line for an hour just to ask a professor a question.

3) ASK IF TUTORS ARE PROVIDED BY THE ATHLETIC DEPARTMENT.

In this day and age of stiff NCAA rules concerning maintenance of academic standards (minimum of 2.0 grade point average for eligibility), most programs are offering tutors at no cost to the athlete. The tutors will usually be paid students but could be a graduate assistant or a fellow player. They will make sure you keep on the books.

4) STUDY TABLE.

Along the same lines as providing tutors, most programs are requiring that all freshman attend study table, or study hall, during the first semester. If you prove yourself academically stable, you are usually relieved of your study table requirements. Those that fail to achieve the minimum academic requirements must continue to attend the early morning study hall. Although this may seem like a minus, it's really a plus to have enforced study hall.

5) MAKE SURE YOU MAY TAKE CLASSES YOU CHOOSE.

Do not allow yourself to be cheated into taking classes designated especially for football players. It is your education and you have the right to take whatever courses you wish. Welcome constructive help from your advisors, but never sell yourself short.

6) COURSE LOADS.

Check out what a school advises as far as course load. A course load is the number of hours per week that you attend classes. The NCAA requires that an athlete take at least twelve class hours per week. Some programs may require as many as sixteen to eighteen hours per week to satisfy that university's own standards. By taking sixteen hours each semester you should be able to graduate in four years.

The Recruiting Survival Guide

7) IS THERE A FULL-TIME ACADEMIC ADVISOR?

Another new dimension to college athletic staffs around the country is academic advisors. These men and women help you design your course loads and choose classes to make the transition from high school to college as smooth as possible. It is also their responsibility to monitor your academic progress toward a degree.

8) GRADUATION RATES.

Check with a coach as to how many players graduate each year. Every successful coach will take pride in attaining that 100% graduation rate. I am proud to say that my class at TCU reached this mark. Check on the graduation rates at the schools you are looking at. The national average for college football players is a disappointing 35%. Don't settle for the dumb jock stereotype.

You will receive a fine education at almost any school you choose, but check out these and other questions you may have first. The bottom line when you finally get to school is that you will get out of your education exactly what you put into it.

Chuck Mooney

19

MAKING THE ACTUAL DECISION

Well you have finally reached it. This is that magic chapter that will clear up each and every question you could possibly have about recruiting. Within this chapter is the infallible formula that will help you make that perfect decision as to which college or university you will attend.

Hogwash.

Coach Steve Brown of TCU was the first to open my eyes to the fact that there is no "perfect" decision. Don't put a ridiculous amount of pressure on yourself by dig-

The Recruiting Survival Guide

ging for every last intangible answer to make the perfect choice. The only thing you'll gain from that is a massive headache and a heck of a lot of stress. When trying to make your decision, you have got to realize that there will be no bad choice. If a school has stayed in your mind this long it is bound to be a good school. Each one of the five may have something different to offer: Family background, success during previous seasons, scenery on campus, head coach, etc. It just depends upon which quality appeals to you the most.

Before you begin to visit schools you must sit down and consider exactly what you are looking for in a school. For me, it was: 1) Academics. 2) Head Coach. 3) A chance to contribute early and 4) How do I feel around the other players?

For everybody it will be different, but some things must be consistent. You must be assured that you will be offered the best opportunity academically. You will hear every statistic imaginable pertaining to studies before this whole thing is over. Coaches will inform you of the number of Academic All-Americans from their schools and the almighty graduation rate. More than once will you hear the words, "Our university has the finest academic program around," and no school is lying. You can get out of school exactly what you put into it, just the same as anything else in life.

Don't put too much emphasis on the campus visit. Don't get me wrong, the visit should have answered a lot of questions for you, but it should not be the only factor in your decision. I would hate to see a football player go off to a school simply because on his visit he partied all night long and met a pretty girl. What you should bring home from the visit is an indication of how much you felt at home with your prospective teammates. Are these the type of guys that you'd like to live and play ball with? How about the head coach? Can you picture yourself playing for him for the next four or five years? Answering questions like these are important, an evaluation of your prospective nightlife is not.

It may be helpful to use a chart and keep score on each school in different categories. This should be a decision aider, not a decision maker. I have included a couple of examples. The first example chart is one that was given to me in 1986 by then-Ohio State assistant coach Randy Hart. The second chart included is one that my father and I used as well.

Once you make your final decision and commit, get excited. Whatever you do, don't look back. Remember that there is no perfect decision, only one that feels right. Now that you've eliminated the stress of deciding on a school, start into your future full speed ahead.

In summary I would say:

1) Don't pressure yourself into looking for the perfect decision.

2) Once you decide, don't look back!

CHOOSING A COLLEGE

COLLEGES

List all of the colleges being considered. In each category below the schools, rate from the best to the worst.

CATEGORIES FOR CONSIDERATION

1. Does the school provide chosen degree or professional career
2. Size (average) of academic classes
3. Are tutors provided by athletic department
4. Is study table required to insure academic success
5. Do you have freedom of choice in class selection
6. Is there a full-time athletic-academic advisor
7. Coaching staff —Quality and number
8. Does program have top administrative support
9. Does program have faculty support
10. Is system of play suited to your abilities
11. Is there an off season program
12. Number of Junior Varsity games
13. Do Freshmen have chance to play varsity
14. Quality of YOUR varsity schedule
15. Opportunity to play based on returning players

16. Dress & grooming regulations - discipline								
17. How do present players feel about coaches and program								
18. Stadium facilities								
19. Locker room facilities								
20. Training room facilities								
21. Dining facilities for athletes								
22. Methods of travel - athletic								
23. Campus setting and atmosphere								
24. Students & athletes - your kind of people								
25. Churches of your choice near to campus								
26. Social opportunities - on & off campus								
27. Summer job help while in college								
28. Job help after graduation								
29. Parents' preference								
30. Number of players in Pro football								
31. Does community support athletic programs								
32. Does Alumni support the University programs								
33. Social and recreational opportunities in the community								
OTHER - fill in as needed:								

The Recruiting Survival Guide

SIMPLE COLLEGE RANKING SHEET

SCHOOL

CRITERIA					
Quality of Education (Importance of Degree)					
Coaching					
Campus/Dorm Life					
Chance for Pro Ball					
Chance to Start 1st or 2nd Year					
National Title Hopes					
Memories/ Family Influence					
Totals					

Chuck Mooney

21

SIGNING DATE

Well, you have now made your decision and the long-awaited day has finally arrived, National Signing Day. This is the day when all the recruits across the country are eligible to sign what is known as a Letter of Intent. This letter with your signature on it obligates you to attend a certain university, and in return the university is obligated to you as well. By just signing your name on this piece of paper, you have saved your folks a bundle of money. Live this day to the fullest because until you graduate or until you marry, this may be your most important day.

The Recruiting Survival Guide

Invite friends and family for the big event. Remember to invite your high school coach as well. Of course your parents or guardian must be on hand to co-sign.

It is also nice to have a camera present to catch the moment on film. If any of the pictures you take have the college coach in them, be sure that they don't appear in your local newspaper because the NCAA frowns upon such exposure. They feel that it is an attempt by the university to sensationalize the event.

The assistant coach who has been recruiting you will then come to your home or school, depending upon what is available in the way of visitation limitations. He will bring copies of a form which entitles you to the actual scholarship. This is known as the "grant-in-aid" form.

Do not feel slighted if the assistant coach is not accompanied by the head coach. The NCAA has instituted restrictions so that the head coach stays in his office all day and fields calls from newly-signed recruits to congratulate them.

You are now officially a member of the team and university with which you have just signed. Get ready for the most exciting, and most challenging four or five years of your life!

Chuck Mooney

22

AFTER IT'S OVER

Welcome back to the real world. Be prepared for your life to slow down dramatically. You have regained your regular-student status. No more reporters will be calling you at night to inquire where you are going. No longer will people stop you on the streets and ask which school you are leaning toward. Never again will a coach come into your home or visit with you at school to try to sell his program. Best of all, you will no longer have to endure hour-long chats with your friendly neighborhood alumni. Your pace of life will slow down drastically. In fact, you will soon be experiencing your first

The Recruiting Survival Guide

weekend at home in a long time. You won't know what to do with a good night's sleep because you have gotten so used to operating on four hours of sleep. Just imagine, after all these busy weeks, you now have a little time to yourself.

You can also begin to overcome your fear of the ringing telephone. I know for a fact that the last few weeks of the recruiting process just about every recruit bolts out of the house with lightning speed at the sound of the ringing telephone. You can now relax and get back to living life like a regular student. Prepare yourself to get back to schoolwork, friends, and family just like a normal kid again.

Don't feel silly about running out to the store and buying every possible sweatshirt, hat, or banner with your school's emblem or logo on it. Let everybody know where you have chosen to go to school. Be proud of your new home.

Now that you have made it through recruiting in one piece, take some time to reflect and rest. Who knows, if you have been taking notes throughout your experience you may want to sit down and write a book!

One last recruiting-related experience may come in the form of a NCAA follow-up interview. This is no big deal. Recently the NCAA has sent special investigators to speak to the top 150 recruits around the country after signing date to make sure all has been fair and legal during the past recruiting season. You will spend up to two hours answering many questions pertaining to four of your five visits. They will ask you to remember dates, times, flight numbers and various other details of your trips. Each visit will basically be reviewed to ensure its legality and the interviewer will check each

Chuck Mooney

school's observation of the rules. Questions will be asked about every visit except the visit to the school with which you eventually signed.

There is nothing to fear during these interviews. Just answer everything to the best of your memory and answer honestly. If you have any questions as to the legality of some of your actions on a trip, call the school in question and talk it over with the coach who recruited you. The interview is nothing to get worked up about, it's just the NCAA's way of policing recruiting.

The Recruiting Survival Guide

22

Thank-You Notes

When all is said and done, and the difficult decision has been made, please take the time to sit down and write thank-you notes to your final five schools. I can't express the importance of a simple note to your recruiter and head coach thanking them for their time. Writing a few words telling them that you appreciated meeting them and visiting their school will say a lot about you. A letter received by the schools you rejected may soften the blow and it is a classy move. Any possible return letter from a coach following your thank-you note makes you feel really good, and reaffirms your belief that you have been dealing with first-rate people throughout the recruiting experience.

The Recruiting Survival Guide

Chuck Mooney

23

GETTING READY FOR YOUR FUTURE

The summer before your first collegiate year is critical. I am writing this chapter five years after having written the previous ones. I want to take the time to tell you the things that no one ever told me before reporting for two-a-days in August.

The Recruiting Survival Guide

The summer before your freshman year, it is of the utmost importance that you train very hard. Lift weights harder than you ever have before. When you report to your new school everyone else will be big and strong. Run harder than ever before, because being in top condition is now more important than ever. Two-a-days will be like nothing you have ever experienced in high school. You will report approximately two weeks before classes begin and you will do nothing all day but eat, sleep, and breathe football. Mom and Dad will no longer be there to greet you when you get home from a hard morning practice.

Only a short nap, a light meal, and a long meeting separate your morning workout from your evening workout. For the first time in your life, you may be physically defeated by an opponent. No matter how much harder you try, the man across from you may beat you over and over again.

This is a shock and is depressing for many players. It was for me. At a time when you need some emotional revamping, it may not be there. The man who was your best friend during recruiting may be the same coach who now chews you out the most and coaches you in a manner that you didn't get in high school. It can be lonely being surrounded by all new faces and sleeping in a strange room on a strange bed.

Many fathers with military experience would compare this time to boot camp. The routines are much the same: Bring in separate members, break them down mentally and physically, push them to exceed their limitations, and then build them back up as a single, fighting unit. This is the time that makes you grow up and become a man. Those who are out of shape can get left behind. Those who cannot adapt emotionally can also be left in the dust.

Coaches have an upcoming season to worry about and cannot afford the time to stop and play psychologist and help pad every young freshman's ego. The ones who are prepared and can adapt will join the rest of the veteran team members and prepare for the first game. The others will spend the remainder of the season fighting to catch up.

What you have just read was cold and callous. It was meant to read that way. You must know that once you report for two-a-days that the party is over. You are no

The Recruiting Survival Guide

longer the media darling, you are now a member of a team.

The coach that recruited you more often than not will have a special interest vested in your personal success due mainly to the fact that during the recruiting months he has returned to the office and professed how great you will be to the other coaches. Therefore, he could be the very same one who works you the hardest and yells at you the most. Never take it personally. It is a business now, not just a game.

No matter how tough your introduction to college football may be, remember that you are not in it alone. There are at least 25 or more incoming freshman experiencing the same feelings. As you will soon find out, the old saying about misery loving company is true. During this time the incoming freshman can become very close and begin bonding.

The key is preparation. Attack two-a-days and start your college career on the right foot. Getting off on the wrong foot can put you in a tough hole to climb out of.

Good luck to all of you, and I hope that there may be a Heismann or Lombardi trophy winner reading the book!